P9-APL-095

Community Questions

WHAT MAKES A COMMUNITY?

by Martha E. H. Rustad

PEBBLE
a capstone imprint

Pebble Emerge is published by Pebble, an imprint of Capstone.
1710 Roe Crest Drive, North Mankato, Minnesota 56003
www.capstonepub.com

Library of Congress Cataloging-in-Publication data is available on the Library of Congress website.
ISBN 978-1-9771-2267-4 (library binding)
ISBN 978-1-9771-2611-5 (paperback)
ISBN 978-1-9771-2294-0 (eBook PDF)
Summary: Despite differences in size, location, and interests, all communities, from urban to rural, share certain characteristics. Through a question-and-answer format and easily relatable photos, young readers learn about community cooperation, responsibility, respect, and the importance of inclusion of all citizens. A simple activity tasks kids with creating their own 3-D community map.

Image Credits
Capstone Studio: Karon Dubke, 20; Getty Images: Hero Images, 11, Purestock, 10; iStockphoto: fstop123, 1, kali9, 13, lechatnoir, 5, OJO Images, 9, SDI Productions, 4 ; Shutterstock: Alex Kravtsov, 19, Alexander Egizarov, 8, DW labs Incorporated, 17, justaa, (icon) cover, Monkey Business Images, Cover, 7, 14, mooremedia, 15, Rawpixel.com, 18, Victoria Kalinina, (pattern) design element, View Apart, 6

Editorial Credits
Editor: Jill Kalz; Designer: Juliette Peters; Media Researcher: Morgan Walters; Production Specialist: Kathy McColley

Printed and bound in China.
3322

Table of Contents

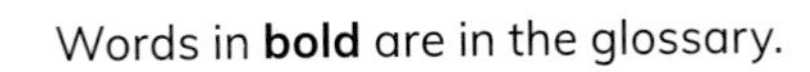

Words in **bold** are in the glossary.

What Is a Community?

A **community** is a group of people. They live together. They work and play together too. Each community is special in its own way.

A community can be any size. Some may be as big as a city. Others may be as small as one room. A community may get bigger or smaller over time.

What Kinds of Communities Are There?

A city is an **urban** community. It has lots of people and buildings. The people live very close to each other. The buildings are also very close to each other.

A **suburban** community is near a city. People live farther apart. Buildings are also farther apart. Trees and grass grow in between.

A **rural** community is far from any cities. People can live very far apart. Buildings can also be very far apart. Trees and grass often cover much of the land.

A community is not always a place. It can be just a group of people. People who love cats can be a community. So can online gamers.

Who Lives in a Community?

You live in a community. The people who live nearby do too. They are your **neighbors**. They may live next door, across the street, or around the corner.

In communities, people share the spaces where they live. People who live in apartments share the same building. A city block is shared by people in their houses.

Neighbors share spaces every day. We go to work and school on shared roads and sidewalks. We may walk, bike, or ride buses together.

People in a community help each other. We follow **rules** to keep everyone safe. Neighbors are kind. They treat others fairly. They make people feel welcome.

STOP

What Does a Community Do?

People work together in a community. Doctors and **nurses** help people stay well. Workers take care of roads. Teachers help people learn. Painters make art to enjoy.

We help our neighbors in many ways. We plant community gardens. We pull weeds and mow grass. We may rake leaves in fall and shovel snow in winter.

Communities share places to play. In parks, we play sports and games. We hike and walk our dogs. We have picnics and listen to music.

People take care of their communities. We pick up trash. We keep things clean. If something is broken, we fix it. We keep each other safe.

People can be part of more than one community. Where you live is one. Another may be your school or where you work. Your classroom is a community.

People in a community share the things they like to do. Some people sing together. Others help at hospitals. Fans cheer for the home team. People make a community!

Get Involved: A 3-D Community Map

Everyone lives in a community. Make a 3-D map of your own town or neighborhood.

What You Need:

- paper and a pencil
- paper bags
- crayons or markers
- old newspapers
- tape
- construction paper
- scissors
- poster paper

What You Do:

1. Make a list of the important buildings and main streets in your community. Are there lakes or rivers nearby?
2. Decorate small paper bags to look like stores or homes. Use large ones to make hospitals, schools, or apartment buildings. Draw windows and doors.
3. Stuff crumpled newspapers inside the bags. Tape the bags shut. Add a construction paper roof or steps.
4. Place the buildings on the poster paper. Draw roads and other landmarks.

Glossary

community (kuh-MYOO-nuh-tee)—a group of people who live, work, and play together

neighbor (NAY-bur)—someone who lives in the same area

nurse (NURSS)—a person trained to take care of sick people, usually in a hospital

rule (ROOL)—a guideline for how to act

rural (RUR-uhl)—away from cities

suburban (suh-BUR-behn)—an area that is away from the center of a city

urban (UR-behn)—having to do with a city

Read More

Emminizer, Theresa. *You're Part of a Neighborhood Community!* New York: Gareth Stevens, 2020.

Keogh, Josie. *What Are Different Types of Communities?* New York: Britannica Educational Publishing, 2018.

Internet Sites

Communities for Kids
https://safeYouTube.net/w/5B7q

Urban, Suburban, Rural
https://www.flocabulary.com/unit/urban-suburban-rural/

Index